FOCKE-WULF Fw 190
THE EARLY YEARS – OPERATIONS IN THE WEST

AIR WAR ARCHIVE

FOCKE-WULF Fw 190

THE EARLY YEARS – OPERATIONS IN THE WEST

CHRIS GOSS

FRONTLINE
BOOKS

FOCKE-WULF Fw 190
The Early Years – Operations in the West

This edition published in 2019 by Frontline Books,
An imprint of Pen & Sword Books Ltd.,
Yorkshire - Philadelphia

ISBN: 978-1-47389-956-8

CIP data records for this title are available from the British Library

Pen & Sword Books Limited incorporates the imprints of Atlas, Archaeology, Aviation, Discovery, Family History, Fiction, History, Maritime, Military, Military Classics, Politics, Select, Transport, True Crime, Air World, Frontline Publishing, Leo Cooper, Remember When, Seaforth Publishing, The Praetorian Press, Wharncliffe Local History, Wharncliffe Transport, Wharncliffe True Crime and White Owl.

PEN & SWORD BOOKS LTD
47 Church Street, Barnsley, South Yorkshire, S70 2AS, England
E-mail: enquiries@pen-and-sword.co.uk
Website: www.pen-and-sword.co.uk

Or
PEN AND SWORD BOOKS
1950 Lawrence Rd, Havertown, PA 19083, USA
E-mail: Uspen-and-sword@casematepublishers.com

For more information on our books, please visit
www.frontline-books.com, email info@frontline-books.com
or write to us at the above address.

Printed and bound by CPI UK

Typeset in 9.5/12pt Avenir by Aura Technology and Software Services, India

CONTENTS

V

PREFACE

I first met former Flight Lieutenant Alfred Price in 1978 before I joined the RAF. We kept in touch over the years, and he, by now Dr Alfred Price, was always free with help and guidance. It therefore came as a shock three years ago when he announced that he was retiring from aviation history writing and moving to be closer to his family in Somerset. At the same time I was honoured that he wanted me to have much of his Luftwaffe material.

It came as an ever greater shock that, finding out three months afterwards that Alfred had passed away on 29 January 2017 aged 81. Since then, I have looked closely at what he left me, which included masses of photographs of Focke-Wulf Fw 190s, his book *Focke-Wulf 190 at War* (Ian Allan Ltd 1977) being one of the first I ever bought. Encouraged by Martin Mace of Frontline Books, I have scanned, with Martin's help, nearly 1,000 Fw 190 photos from both my collection and Alfred's. The aim is now to produce two photo books with at least 200 photos per book with full captions illustrating this enigmatic fighter. The books are not intended to be an in-depth study of the aircraft and its operational history, but they are intended as a tribute to the work done by Dr Alfred Price.

Chris Goss, Marlow, 2019

INTRODUCTION

In late 1937, the Reichsluftfahrtministerium placed a development contract with the Focke-Wulf Flugzeugbau GmbH for a new single-seat fighter which would eventually replace the Messerschmitt 109.

A series of design proposals were submitted to the ministry, most of which included the aircraft being powered by a liquid-cooled inline engine. However, Dipl. Ing. Kurt Tank, Focke-Wulf's Technical Director, proposed the aircraft be powered by an air-cooled radial engine using the powerful BMW 139. Tank successfully persuaded the Reichsluftfahrtministerium, which in 1938 issued a contract for three prototypes of what would be called the Fw 190. In keeping with tradition, Focke-Wulf also gave the aircraft the name of a bird of prey, in this case Würger or Butcher Bird/Shrike.

The first prototype, the Fw 190 V1 coded D-OPZE, featured a ducted spinner and first flew from the Neuenlander Feld on 1 June 1939 with Flugkapitän Hans Sander, Focke-Wulf's chief test pilot, at the controls. Apart from minor technical concerns, the aircraft was shown to have good manoeuvrability, good control response, a high rate of roll and a good diving speed. However, the BMW 139 engine was prone to overheating, even with the ducted spinner removed, so it was decided to fit the fifth prototype with the better, albeit bigger and heavier, BMW 801. As a result, airframe changes were made which included a smaller wing (V5k) and larger wing (V5g). Whilst testing continued, construction of forty pre-production aircraft (the A-0) began and in March 1941, six aircraft were assigned to the Erprobungsstaffel 190, the unit responsible for operationally testing the Fw 190, at Rechlin-Roggenthin. This unit was essentially made up from elements of II./Jagdgeschwader 26 and was commanded by Oberleutnant Otto Behrens.

It was the Fw 190 A-1 that would now be tested under operational conditions. It was armed with four 7.92mm MG 17s (two in the front fuselage and two in the wing roots) with two 20mm MG FF cannon fitted outboard on the wing. This was quickly followed by the A-2 which saw the two inboard MG 17 machine guns replaced with two MG FF cannon. However, the BMW 801C engine still suffered from overheating and the cannon had a slow rate of fire, so this resulted in the A-3 with the BMW 801D engine, the MG FF cannon moved outboard and the improved 20mm MG 151 fitted in the inboard positions.

In July 1941, Erprobungsstaffel 190 moved from Rechlin to Le Bourget near Paris and began converting II Gruppe/Jagdgeschwader 26, commanded by Ritterkreuz holder Hauptmann Walter Adolph, to the Fw 190 starting with Oberleutnant Walter Schneider's 6 Staffel. By the start of

September 1941, all of II Gruppe had converted but it is believed that the first combat was in the early morning of 16 August 1941 when Hauptmann Adolph led a mixed Fw 190/Bf 109 formation and claimed to have shot down four Spitfires. The first Fw 190 to be lost was on 21 August 1941 when Oberfeldwebel Walter Meyer of 6./Jagdgeschwader 26 suffered engine failure and on 29 August 1941 Leutnant Heinz Schenk, also from 6 Staffel, was shot down and killed by German Flak.

RAF pilots soon reported encountering radial-engined fighters over France, thinking that they were ex-French Air Force Curtis Hawk 75s but as one RAF pilot noted 'No Hawk ever had the performance of that brute!'. They soon realized that they were up against the Fw 190.

The first combat loss of an Fw 190 occurred at 1050hrs on 18 September 1941. Scrambled to intercept Bristol Blenheims attacking a convoy off Ostend, Walter Adolph led II./Jagdgeschwader 26 to intercept. Pilot Officer Cyril Babbage of 41 Squadron records what happened:

> . . . . this enemy aircraft appeared to be similar to the Curtiss 75A but with slimmer fuselage. The enemy passed beneath me and I saw crosses on the fuselage. It then turned south at high speed and I followed it . . . I got within range just off Ostende and fired a five second burst with cannon and machine guns from dead astern. The enemy aircraft broke up and crashed into the sea . . .

The body of Walter Adolph, who had one victory in Spain and twenty-four in the Second World War, was washed ashore the following month.

As 1941 progressed, the remaining Gruppe from Jagdgeschwader 26 converted to the Fw 190, followed in 1942 by Jagdgeschwader 2. RAF pilots were finding how inferior their fighters now were, especially when the Fw 190 was flown by an experienced pilot but with the Fw 190 still operating over Europe and the Channel, the RAF still knew little about the intricacies of this German fighter. This would all change on 23 June 1942.

Early that evening, six Douglas Bostons of 107 Squadron took off from Exeter to attack a target at Morlaix in Brittany, escort being provided by Spitfires of the Perranporth and Exeter Wings. At Cherbourg-Maupertus, Fw 190s of III./Jagdgeschwader 2 were scrambled and followed the RAF back to the Devon coast where they pounced. One Fw 190 collided with the Exeter Wing Leader, the pilot of the former, Unteroffizier Willi Reuschling of 7./Jagdgeschwader 2, baling out to be captured, the pilot of the latter, Wing Commander Alois Vasatko, being killed. A series of dogfights then ensued with the RAF coming off worse. Oberleutnant Armin Faber of Stab III./Jagdgeschwader 2 shot down a Spitfire of 310 Squadron and probably damaged another from 19 Squadron after which he apparently became disorientated and landed his Fw 190 A-3 at RAF Pembrey in South Wales, presenting the RAF with a pristine example of the fighter which would be comprehensively evaluated.

Despite the secrets of the Fw 190 being revealed at last, very few Fw 190s operating in the pure fighter role would be seen or even lost over Britain. A few Störangriff (nuisance attacks) were carried out by Fw 190s, attacking targets at high speed and low level using gunfire but the first Fw 190 was not lost on such a mission until 21 October 1942 when Feldwebel Werner Brychy of 4./Jagdgeschwader 2 flew into a fog-shrouded hillside at Lulworth in Dorset. Then on 31 October 1942, Feldwebel Alfred Hell of 5./Jagdgeschwader 2 was shot down by anti-aircraft fire and captured at Sandwich in Kent whilst escorting a fighter-bomber attack on Canterbury. The final Fw 190 operating as a pure fighter to come down on land did so in quite spectacular fashion on 27 November 1942 when Oberfeldwebel Heinz Bierwith of 5./Jagdgeschwader 26 collided with a train he was strafing at Lydd station; he was killed instantly. Such attacks would continue sporadically but far more Fw 190s would be seen over Britain engaged on other types of missions. By the end of 1942, I and II./Jagdgeschwader 2 had moved to operate over the Mediterranean in response to the Allied landings in North Africa in November 1942. II Gruppe would be the last to return to northern France in March 1943.

Fitting bombs to fighters started in the Battle of Britain but by 1941, interest in Jagdbomber (fighter-bomber) or Jabo missions had become secondary and only then against shipping. However, Oberleutnant Frank Liesendahl of Jagdgeschwader 2 convinced the Luftwaffe to form a dedicated Jabostaffel flying the Bf 109 F. Liesendahl was so successful that in March 1942, the Jabostaffel became 10.(Jabo)/Jagdgeschwader 2 and Jagdgeschwader 26 was ordered to form its own 10 Staffel.

In June 1942, both Jabostaffel moved to Le Bourget to convert to the Fw 190. This was worrying for the RAF as the Fw 190 had already proven itself superior in all flight parameters (apart from turning radius) to the Spitfire Mark Vb, being 30mph faster and having the highest rate of roll of any fighter of the Second World War. It could also carry a single 500kg bomb under the fuselage and four 50kg bombs under the wings, twice the bombload of a Bf 109 F.

The first Fw 190 Jabo attack took place against shipping on 7 July 1942 and from now on, at least one such attack a day was planned, weather and serviceability permitting. Attacks now began with virtual impunity, albeit by the end of the month two Staffelkapitän had been lost with 10./Jagdgeschwader 2 losing Hauptmann Frank Liesendahl attacking a ship off Brixham on 17 July 1942 and 10./Jagdgeschwader 26 losing Oberleutnant Hans-Joachim Geburtig off Littlehampton on 30 July 1942. Liesendahl was killed and was awarded the Ritterkreuz posthumously whilst Geburtig was captured.

The first Fw 190 Jabo crashed on land on 26 August 1942. Two aircraft of 10./Jagdgeschwader 26, flown by Obergefreiter Richard Wittmann and Oberfeldwebel Werner Kassa, attacked industrial targets in Eastbourne but as Kassa banked away after dropping his bomb, he presented a much better target for a machine-gunner on a factory roof. Kassa lost control, continued rolling and hit the ground inverted, killing him instantly.

By the end of 1942, 10./Jagdgeschwader 2 had lost three Jabos of which just one had crashed on land whilst 10./Jagdgeschwader 26 had lost seven with two crashing on land. Both units now began switching from attacking shipping and coastal targets to targets inland. Another change was a massed vengeance attack against Canterbury on 31 October 1942 with 70 per cent of the bombs landing on target for just one escort fighter shot down by Flak. To add insult to injury, two RAF fighters were also shot down by German fighters. This was the precursor for another vengeance attack against eastern London on 20 January 1943 by twenty-eight Jabos. Just one Fw 190 of 10./Jagdgeschwader 26 flown by Leutnant Hermann Hoch was lost to anti-aircraft fire on the way home, Hoch being captured.

The British now increased their fighter, balloon and gun defences but still attacks occurred from as far east as Suffolk to as far west as Cornwall. A new Jabo unit, Schnellkampfgeschwader 10, became operational at the start of March 1943 after which it subsumed 10./Jagdgeschwader 2 and 10./Jagdgeschwader 26. With nearly 120 Jabos available by mid-April 1943, it came as a great surprise that the vast majority were to be used for nocturnal attacks and as a result, daylight attacks soon declined.

The first nocturnal attack on the night of 16–17 April 1943 was a farce. Two aircraft were lost during the day with one pilot killed, then three Fw 190s collided taking off for the mission with one pilot killed whilst two more suffered take-off accidents. Over Britain, four pilots became disorientated with one being killed when his aircraft ran out of fuel, the remaining three landing or trying to land at RAF West Malling in Kent. A final pilot disappeared – the total cost for the night being ten aircraft destroyed, two damaged, four pilots killed and three captured.

Understandably, there was a break of a month in nocturnal attacks whilst May 1943 saw twelve daylight attacks on seven days. However, the attack on Eastbourne in the early afternoon of 6 June 1943 was the last daylight Jabo attack on Britain of the war. II./Schnellkampfgeschwader 10 now moved to the Mediterranean, leaving I./Schnellkampfgeschwader 10 to carry out nocturnal attacks which it did until the night of 5 June 1944 after which it operated solely over Normandy following the Allied invasion, being re-designated III./Kampfgeschwader 51.

Luftwaffe reconnaissance missions were normally carried out by twin-engined aircraft but from as early as July 1941, 1 Staffel (Fern)/Aufklärungsgruppe 123 also had around five Bf 109s. The first loss over the UK was due to engine failure on 7 January 1942 and the first combat loss being on 24 April 1942 off Portland. As the year progressed, 3.(Fern)/Aufklärungsgruppe 123, 4.(Fern)/Aufklärungsgruppe 123 and 1.(Fern)/Aufklärungsgruppe 122 began flying limited missions over the UK but on 19 December 1942, 3.(Fern)/Aufklärungsgruppe 122 reported the first loss of an Fw 190 A-3 when Feldwebel Paul Gellert was shot down 30 miles south of Shoreham by a Typhoon of 486 Squadron.

By 1943, both 4. and 5.(Fern)/Aufklärungsgruppe 123 (formed in November 1942) reported having a few Fw 190s on strength but the only recorded combat loss of an Fw 190 was from 5.(Fern)/Aufklärungsgruppe 123 on 13 March 1943 when Feldwebel Oskar Sahre was shot down and killed by a Typhoon of 1 Squadron off Beachy Head. However, the major user of the Fw 190 for reconnaissance over the UK was Nahaufklärungsgruppe 13 which was formed late in 1942. It consisted 1 and 2 Staffel (3 Staffel did not form until spring 1944, too late to operate over the UK), and its first combat loss, flying from St Brieuc in Brittany, was not until 30 July 1943 when Oberleutnant Rainer Einhardt and Oberfeldwebel Werner Schröder of 2 Staffel were shot down off Plymouth by Spitfires of 165 Squadron. Just two more were lost before the end of 1943, the last mention of an Fw 190 being on 20 November 1943 when Unteroffizier Hermann Oettinger of 1 Staffel was wounded off Start Point by Spitfires of 610 Squadron. In 1944, the Bf 109 G-5 and G-6 appears to have replaced the Fw 190 as no more were recorded lost in combat or accidents in operations over the UK.

FW 190 OPERATIONAL VARIANTS

Variant	Engine	Armament	Other Changes
A-1	BMW 801 C-1	4 x 7.92mm MG 17, 2 x 20mm MG FF	
A-2	BMW 801 C-2	2 x 7.92mm MG 17, 2 x 20mm MG 151/20, 2 x 20mm MG FF	As A-1; wingspan increased
A-3	BMW 801 D-2	"	As A-2
A-4	"	"	Radio upgrade, supplementary fuel injection system
A-5	"	"	Lengthened fuselage due to redesigned engine mounting, application of Umbau Rüstsätze such as cameras
A-6	"	2 x 7.92mm MG 17, 4 x 20mm MG 151/20	Modified wing & armament, application of Umbau Rüstsätze

Variant	Engine	Armament	Other Changes
A-7	BMW 801 D-2	2 x 13mm MG 131, 4 x 20mm MG 151/20	As A-6
A-8	"	2 x 13mm MG 131, 4 x 20mm MG 151/20, optionally 2 x 13mm MG 131, 2 20mm MG 151/20 2 x 30mm MK 108	Radio upgrade, repositioned bomb rack
D-9	Jumo 213 A	2 x 13mm MG 131, 2 x 20mm MG 151/20	
F-1	BMW 801 D-2	2 x 7.92mm MG 17, 2 x 20mm MG 151/20	Jabo based on A-4
F-2	"	"	Jabo based on A-5. Improved canopy
F-3	"	"	Jabo based on A-6
F-8	"	2 x 13mm MG 131, 2 x 20mm MG 151/20	Jabo based on A-8
F-9	BMW 801 TS	"	Jabo
G-1	BMW 801 D-2	2 x 20mm MG 151/20	Long-range Jabo based on A-4
G-2	"	"	As G-1 based on A-5
G-3	"	"	As G-2 with autopilot PKS 11
G-8	"	"	As G-2 based on A-8

A wartime-enhanced photograph of an Fw 190 A-8 believed to be from 6./Jagdgeschwader 1. Where the photographer possibly went wrong is when the canopy is closed, the step retracts unless in this case there has been a malfunction.

This A-1/U1 Jabo is carrying a single 250kg bomb.

Opposite above: A mechanic carrying out engine runs on an Fw 190 A-1 of an unidentified unit, France 1941–2. The 17 is believed to be yellow and the partial stylized eagle after the engine exhausts have been associated with III./Jagdgeschwader 2.

Opposite below: The Fw 190 proved to be an ideal Jabo. This aircraft, an Fw 190 A-1/U1, appears to have the last two digits of its werk nummer 0098 below the front of the canopy, is carrying a single 50kg bomb under the wing and at least two under the fuselage.

The end – the remains of an Fw 190 showing the bomb racks for 250kg bombs. The aircraft appears to have been destroyed *in situ* as there is no evidence of an engine and the spinner lies underneath the wing.

Opposite: What appears to be an A-4 F-8 Jabo with a single AB250-2/224 SD1 container which held 224 SD1 anti-personnel bomblets.

GLOSSARY

Aufklärer	Reconnaissance
Bf	Bayerische Flugzeugwerke (Prefix for Messerschmitt Bf 109 & 110)
Deutsches Kreuz in Gold	German Cross in Gold
Ehrenpokal	Goblet of Honour – awarded for outstanding achievements in the air war
Eiserne Kreuz	Iron Cross (came in First and Second Class)
Ergänzungs	Training
Erprobungs	Experimental
Fähnrich/Oberfähnrich	Officer Cadet/Senior Officer Cadet
Feldwebel	Flight Sergeant
Fern	Long-range
Flak	Anti-aircraft
Führer	Leader
Gefreiter	Leading Aircraftman
Geschwader	Group consisting three Gruppen commanded by a Geschwader Kommodore
Gruppe	Wing consisting three Staffeln; commanded by a Gruppen Kommandeur. Gruppe number denoted by Roman numerals (e.g. II)
Hauptmann	Flight Lieutenant/Captain
Ia	Operations Officer
Jabo	Fighter-bomber
Jagdfliegerschule	Fighter Pilot School
Jagdgeschwader	Fighter Group
Jagdgruppe	Fighter Wing
Kampfgeschwader	Bomber Group
Leutnant	Pilot Officer/2nd Lieutenant
Major	Squadron Leader/Major
Nachtschlachtgruppe	Night Ground-attack Wing
Nahaufklärungsgruppe	Short-range reconnaissance Wing
Oberfeldwebel	Warrant Officer

Obergefreiter	Senior Aircraftman/Corporal
Oberleutnant	Flying Officer/1st Lieutenant
Reichsluftfahrtministerium	Air Ministry
Ritterkreuz	Knight's Cross
Ritterkreuz mit Eichenlaub	Knight's Cross with Oak Leaves
Schlachtgeschwader	Ground-attack Group
Schnell	Fast
Sonderfstaffel	Special Squadron
Stab	Staff or HQ; formation in which Gruppen Kommandeur and Geschwader Kommodore flew
Staffel	Squadron (twelve aircraft); commanded by a Staffel Kapitän (St Kap). Staffel number denoted by Arabic numerals (e.g. 2)
stammkennzeichen	Factory code
Umbau Rüstsätze	Field or factory modification
Unteroffizier	Sergeant
werk nummer	Serial Number
Zerstörer	Destroyer/Heavy fighter
Zerstörergeschwader	Heavy Fighter Group

TRAINING

A Focke-Wulf Flugzeugbau advert for its new single-seat fighter.

Opposite above: The personnel of Focke Wulf's Industrie Schutzstaffel are visited by ace Major Walter Nowotny (second from right) who by the time of his death on 8 November 1944 had been credited with 258 kills. With him are (left to right): Oberfeldwebel Hans Kampmeier, Werner Finke, Oberfeldwebel Rolf Mondry and (far right) Alfred Motsch. Kampmeier was injured on 8 March 1944 in Fw 190A-5/U10 werk nummer 150861 coded BP+LY when he force-landed at Hannover-Langenhagen after combat; he was credited with a B-17 on 28 July 1943. Finke was killed in 1944 testing an Fw 190 D-9. Mondry had flown with 7./Jagdgeschwader 26 in 1941–2, where he scored two kills and was injured in an accident on 5 April 1942 at Gravelines in France. He claimed a B-17 on 8 October 1943 but was then wounded in an air attack on Langenhagen on 8 March 1944, losing an arm. Motsch was injured on 9 October 1943 when he force-landed his Fw 190 A-4, werk nummer 145631 Black 3, at Helgoland.

Opposite below: An Fw 190 A-4 of an unidentified unit has come to grief, looking as if the cause was a boggy airfield.

An unusual photograph. Hard to work out which way up it is but the suspension cables give it away. This is Fw 190 V5 werk nummer 0005, the fifth prototype powered by a BMW 801 C-0 engine. It is further designated V5g as it has a longer wingspan. V5k would indicated a shorter wingspan.

Same aircraft showing the code Black 7. Also visible is the first aid access panel and the remains of the stammkennzeichen or factory code on the fuselage to the right of the cross. The flaps are down indicating the aircraft was probably in the process of landing.

Unteroffizier Werner Schammert joined 10.(Jabo)/Jagdgeschwader 26 in the latter half of 1942 from Jagdgruppe West in Cazaux where this photograph was taken. He would be shot down by anti-aircraft fire attacking RAF Manston on 10 October 1942; he baled out injured and his Fw 190 A-3 werk nummer 0420 coded 7+< crashed into houses at Ramsgate in Kent.

A spectacular accident to an Fw 190 A-3 coded Red 21 of Jagdgruppe West, 1942. Damage would appear to be slight.

View of Red 21 from the starboard side showing damage to the airscrew. It would appear the pilot was uninjured so records of this accident would be hard to find.

Werner Schammert in the cockpit of White 18 at Cazaux, 1942.

Opposite: This view of Red 21 shows more serious damage to the port wing, which would result in a wing change.

Opposite: Werner Schammert is wearing a one-piece flying suit and kapok life jacket. Hanging from the life jacket is a packed of fluorescent dye. Cazaux was located near to the coast so there would have been training flights over water.

Werner Schammert in the cockpit of his Fw 190. He is wearing a netzkopfhaube flying helmet and splitterbrille glasses.

Oberfähnrich Helmut Wenk joined Ergänzungs/Schnellkampfgeschwader 10 at Cognac in Spring 1943. He would be posted to 6./Schnellkampfgeschwader 10 the following month and after having flown just one mission over the UK, moved with his Staffel to the Mediterranean.

Helmut Wenk standing next to Fw 190 A-3 werk nummer 5381 code White 7. He is wearing a netzkopfhaube flying helmet but does not appear to have a life jacket under his parachute harness.

Opposite above: A head-on view of Fw 190 A-3 werk nummer 5381. To the right is a refueller, to the left what the RAF would call a 'Trolley Acc', providing electrical power to start the aircraft.

Opposite below: A good port-side view of Fw 190 A-3 werk nummer 5381. Note the mechanic with his foot on the ladder.

Helmut Wenk in the cockpit of werk nummer 5381. This aircraft suffered engine failure on a training flight on 4 June 1943 and the unknown pilot baled out, the aircraft crashing 4km north of Bordeaux at 1235hrs.

Unteroffizer Heinz Ehrhardt converting to the Fw 190 after which he would fly the aircraft in the Jabo role. Here he is undergoing training after which he joined 2./Schnellkampfgeschwader 10 and he would land his Fw 190 in error at RAF Manston on 20 May 1943 during an operational night mission. There is disagreement as to whether this is Ehrhardt in the aircraft as DT+FO is believed to have been a F-8 which did not come into service until after Ehrhardt was captured. Others believe that this is an A-4 – no under-wing bomb racks as fitted to the F-8 are visible, the profile of the upper fuselage forward of the cockpit is that of an Fw 190 prior to the A-5 or F-8 series, i.e. an airplane fitted with MG 17s, the very rear end of the teardrop-shaped fairing on the lower cowling goes slightly back beyond and over the wing fillet as characteristic of the A-4 (the lengthened fuselage of the A-5 and later and of the F-8 shifted the teardrop fairing forward about 6in, or forward of the wing fillet).

THE PEMBREY 190

Ace Oberleutnant Egon Mayer, Staffekapitän of 7./Jagdgeschwader 2, led the bounce on the Perranporth and Exeter Wings on 23 June 1942, claiming his 47th and 48th victories that evening. He would be killed in action commanding Jagdgeschwader 2 on 2 March 1944 with his score standing at 102.

Opposite: Willi Reuschling seen here as a POW in Canada. He had already shot down a Whirlwind and a Hudson before colliding with the Spitfire flown by Wing Commander Vasatko.

Below: Wing Commander Alois Vasatko had commanded the Exeter Wing since April 1942. He had flown with the French Air Force in the Battle of France, being credited with being involved with twelve aircraft destroyed and two probables. He then escaped to England and joined 312 Squadron, taking command of the Squadron in July 1941. At the time of his death, his score stood at four and ten shared destroyed, two and two shared probables and one damaged, his last 'victory' being the Fw 190 flown by Unteroffizier Willi Reuschling. (via Popelka)

Above: Understandably, the arrival of Oberleutnant Faber's Fw 190 created considerable interest. The aircraft has the III./Jagdgeschwader 2 cockerel's head on the cowling, the Gruppen Adjutant's chevron on the fuselage and the *werk nummer* on the top of the tail. Despite Faber claiming four victories, unusually none are recorded on this aircraft possibly casting doubt on his claims. Note the 234 Squadron Spitfire in the background, this squadron being based at Portreath in Cornwall at this time.

Below: Work has started on the Fw 190 whilst still at Pembrey. Note the sentry in the background.

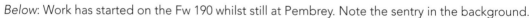

Group Captain John Grandy (Station Commander RAF Duxford), Squadron Leader Philip Lucas (Hawker test pilot) and Group Captain Richard Atcherly (Station Commander RAF Fairwood Common) take a closer look at the Fw 190's BMW 801 engine.

Perfect side view showing the un-stylized black area behind the exhaust. Note the Blenheim Mk I in the background.

Opposite above: Close-up of the engine-mounted twin 7.92mm MG 17s.

Opposite below: With almost all panels open, more and more people pore over the Fw 190 A-3.

Opposite above: Starboard view; in the background there appears to be a mix of Beaufighters and Blenheims.

Opposite below: The rudder clearly shows no sign of Faber's alleged four victories.

Good view from the front starboard quarter showing clearly the wing armament of the Fw 190 A-3.

RAF aircrew now have the opportunity to have a closer look at an aircraft which they first encountered in August 1941.

Opposite above: The mess made by the exhausts is evident in this photograph.

Opposite below: Poorer-quality photo showing the standard wing camouflage.

Opposite above: The view from the starboard side – the stand on the port side still allows aircrew to view the pristine aircraft while minimizing the chance of damage to a still-airworthy aircraft.

Opposite below: The Fw 190 was transported by road to RAE Farnborough, arriving on or around 29 June 1942 as from that date on, HQ Fighter Command warned all air-defence units that a captured Fw 190 would be operating from Farnborough both with and without a Spitfire escort. Allocated the serial MP499 and marked with a yellow P, its German markings were obliterated. It was first flown by Wing Commander Hugh 'Willie' Wilson on 3 July 1942 after which comprehensive testing was carried out.

The cockpit of werk nummer 313 is of particular interest.

Cockpit view right.

Opposite: Cockpit view looking forward; note how new the cockpit appears.

Cockpit view left.

Airborne in new markings.

Head-on but with British markings.

Undergoing trials – the under-surfaces were yellow.

Opposite: With no spinner, compared to earlier photographs the engine appears to have been cleaned up following capture.

Cockpit clearly showing the good visibility that Fw 190 pilots enjoyed.

Opposite above: Under the starboard wing showing the flaps; note the engine panels to the right are all open and the cartridge ejection port ahead of the flaps.

Opposite below: The Fw 190 A-3 has been camouflaged dark green and dark earth on the upper surfaces but the III./Jagdgeschwader 2 badge remains.

Underneath the port wing. Note the pressure stencilled on the undercarriage jack, the guns are still *in situ* and to the left, the cartridge ejection port.

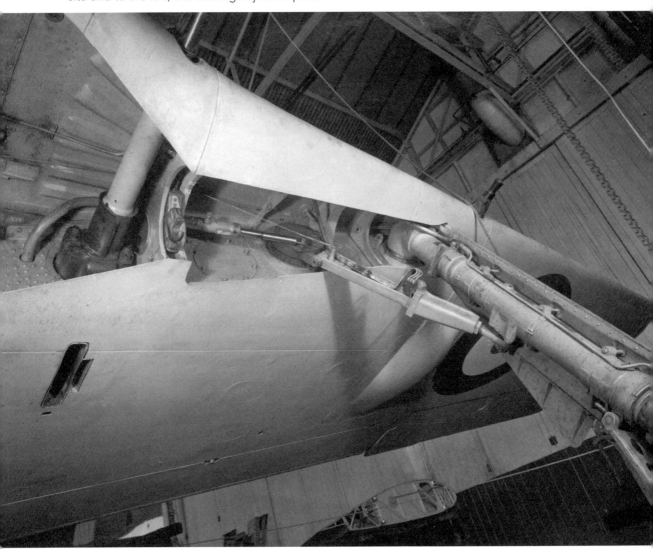

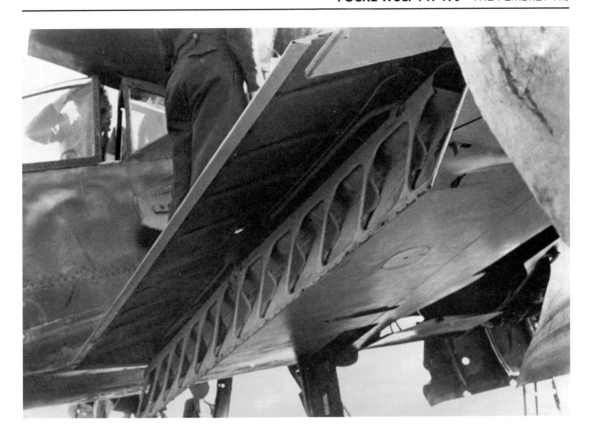

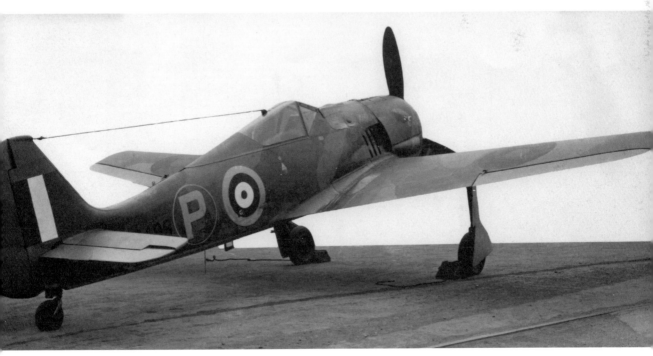

Werk nummer 313's BMW 801 showing also the MG 151 and MG FF guns in the wing.

The engine has been removed but the werk nummer 313 is stencilled on the firewall. The last recorded flight of 313 was 29 January 1943 and the aircraft struck off charge on 18 September 1943.

JAGDGESCHWADER 2

Pilots of 10. (Jabo)/Jagdgeschwader 2 converting from the Bf 109 F-4 to the Fw 190 at Le Bourget in June 1942. Left is Leutnant Leopold Wenger who would be awarded the Deutsches Kreuz in Gold in October 1943 and the Ritterkreuz in January 1945, only to be killed in action on 10 April that year. To the right is Oberfeldwebel Gerhard Limburg who would be awarded the Ehrenpokal in July 1943 by which time he had been promoted to Leutnant and the Deutsches Kreuz in Gold in March 1944; he would survive the war.

Opposite above: Fw 190 A-s of Oberleutnant Erich Rudorffer's 6./Jagdgeschwader 2 at Beaumont-Le-Roger, early 1942. It would appear that II./Jagdgeschwader 2 is still operating the Bf 109 F: the tail of one is in the foreground and another in the distance.

Opposite below: An Fw 190 A-3 of 9./Jagdgeschwader 2 photographed at Vannes, 1942. Note the stylizing of the black behind the exhausts and the adoption of the III./Jagdgeschwader 2 cockerel's head

Brand-new Fw 190s at Le Bourget ready to convert pilots to the new type.

Believed to be the Fw 190 A-3 of Oberleutnant Egon Mayer of 7./Jagdgeschwader 2. He took command of III./Jagdgeschwader 2 from Hauptmann Hans 'Assi' Hahn at the start of November 1942 by which time his score stood at fifty-two, his last kill with 7 Staffel being a Spitfire on 19 August 1942. His next kill was a B-17 on 23 November 1942. Command of 7./Jagdgeschwader 2 then went to Hauptmann Erich Hohagen.

Opposite above: A poor photo of 7./Jagdgeschwader 2 over western France during the summer of 1943. By this time 7 Staffel was subordinate to II./Jagdgeschwader 2, fighter Gruppe having been increased from three to four Staffel. The Staffelkapitän by this time were Oberleutnant Kurt Bühligen (to the end of June 1943), Leutnant Werner Beckers (killed 8 September 1943) and Leutnant Wilhelm Felgel von Farnholz (killed 26 November 1943).

Opposite below: An Fw 190 A-3 coded White 6+I of 7./Jagdgeschwader 2. This aircraft was flown regularly by Unteroffizier Otto Kleinert. Kleinert would shoot down a Spitfire on 15 February 1943 and a B-17 on 1 May 1943, with another B-17 unconfirmed on 6 March 1943. He was shot down in combat on 16 August 1943, baling out of his Fw 190 A-5/U12 werk nummer 1167 near Pontoise, and would survive the war.

Pilots of 7./Jagdgeschwader 2 with their old and new Staffelkapitän at Brest or Vannes, November 1942. Left to right: Unteroffizier Wolfgang Ortlepp (wounded 19 November 1944), Unteroffizier Friedrich, Unteroffizier Wilhelm Scherwadt, Leutnant Werner Dahms, Hauptmann Egon Mayer, Engelhardt, Hauptmann Erich Hohagen, Leutnant Fritz Holzapfel (+ 19 July 1943), Unteroffizier Werner Beckers (+ 8 September 1943), Feldwebel Kurt Knappe (+ 3 September 1943), Oberfeldwebel Alfred Knies (wounded 26 November 1943), Unteroffizier Otto Kleinert.

Opposite above: This Fw 190 A of 7./Jagdgeschwader 2 has suffered an undercarriage problem. It is possible that this is A-2 werk nummer 0333 which suffered an accident at Théville on 29 July 1942. Repaired, this aircraft was then shot down while attacking B-17s on 21 October 1942, Oberleutnant Otto Lutter being killed in the crash at Douarenez

Opposite below: Fw 190 A of 7./Jagdgeschwader 2, werk nummer 0205 coded White 4+I suffered an engine failure on 16 October 1942 and was severely damaged crash-landing at Brest-Nord.

Oberfeldwebel Georg Keil of 3./Jagdgeschwader 2 seen at Caen in 1942. He was credited with two victories on 19 August 1942 after which he was apparently posted to Jagdgeschwader 11. On 24 December 1944 an Oberfeldwebel Georg Keil with 5./Jagdgeschwader 11 was awarded the Deutsches Kreuz in Gold. Some confusion exists about this pilot as there was a Feldwebel Günther Keil with 2./Jagdgeschwader 2 (eight kills, + 20 June 1942), a Oberfeldwebel Keil with 11./Jagdgeschwader 301 in 1944 and an Oberfeldwebel Georg Kiel with 8 and 9./Jagdgeschwader 11 in 1943–4.

Opposite: Feldwebel Willi Morzinek of 1./Jagdgeschwader 2 and his mechanic. Morzinek flew his first mission with 4./Jagdgeschwader 2 on 14 October 1940. He converted to the Fw 190 in April–May 1942 and flew his last operational flight on 8 April 1945 by which time his score of victories stood at 15½.

Oberleutnant Bruno Stolle was the Staffelkapitän of 8./Jagdgeschwader 2 until taking command of III./Jagdgeschwader 2 from Hauptmann Egon Mayer at the end of June 1943. His first kill was with 8./Jagdgeschwader 2 on 11 August 1940: his last kill with 8./Jagdgeschwader 2 was his 34th on 29 May 1943. His first as Gruppen Kommandeur was not until 30 December 1943 and would be his last of the war. He would be awarded the Ritterkreuz on 17 March 1943 and survived the war. Note the map of Brittany on his left knee.

Opposite: Leutnant Friedrich Fleischmann of 9./Jagdgeschwader 2 climbs out of Yellow 9+I. He had the one kill, a B-17 on 4 July 1943 but eleven days later his Fw 190 A-5 werk nummer 7318 suffered engine failure and he was injured in the ensuing forced- landing at Vannes. Note the less bulky life jacket and the signal flares strapped to his left boot.

Opposite: Final adjustments to Bruno Stolle's parachute. Note the Fw 190 in the background is coded with what would appear to be White 24 whilst other photos show the III./Jagdgeschwader 2 vertical band around the rear of the fuselage.

Bruno Stolle getting into the cockpit of his Fw 190, Brest 1942. Note the fuel octane triangle.

Opposite above: Believed to be Unteroffizier Rudolf Eisele of 8./Jagdgeschwader 2 getting out of his Fw 190 at Brest, late 1942–early 1943. His first victory was a Spitfire of 133 Squadron on 26 September 1942 and by the end of that year, his score had risen to seven. He would be promoted to Feldwebel then Oberfeldwebel early 1943, getting his first kill of the year on January 6 (a Whitley of 10 Operational Training Unit). However, he would only be credited with one more kill (a Spitfire on 26 January 1943) before his Fw 190 A-5 werk nummer 2634 was shot down by German Flak over Brest harbour on 14 April 1943 and he was killed.

Opposite below: Fw 190 A-2 werk nummer 2154, coded White 7 of 7./Jagdgeschwader 2. This aircraft was damaged in an accident at Théville on 31 July 1942, suffering 30 per cent damage.

White 24 has the III./Jagdgeschwader 2 black painting behind the exhausts.

Opposite above: 7./Jagdgeschwader 2 photographed at Vannes March–April 1942. Note that White 7+I (*werk nummer* 435 being the aircraft favoured by Egon Mayer) has the 7 Staffel top hat and thumb badge as opposed to the cockerel's head. Left to right: Unteroffizier Wolfgang Orlepp (wounded 19 November 1944), Unteroffizier Friedrich, Oberfeldwebel Alfred Knies (wounded 26 November 1943), Unteroffizier Wilhelm Scherwadt, Oberfeldwebel Fritz Schneidewind (wounded 1 December 1943), Leutnant Werner Dahms, Hauptmann Erich Hohagen (Staffelkapitän until 6 April 1943), Leutnant Friedrich Holzapfel (+ 19 July 1943), Unteroffizier Werner Beckers (+ 8 September 1943), Unteroffizier Martin Mohn (+ 1 December 1943), Unteroffizier Otto Kleinert.

Opposite below: A very young-looking Unteroffizier Otto Kleinert of 7./Jagdgeschwader 2 at Cherbourg, summer 1942. The aircraft is an A-2/A-3 variant and note the 7./Jagdgeschwader 2 badge on the cowling. Again, the black area behind the exhausts has been outlined in white.

Two unidentified pilots of 8./Jagdgeschwader 2 stage a practice 'alarmstart' at what is believed to be Brest, late 1942–early 1943. Nearest aircraft is an Fw 190 A-3 werk nummer 2181 Black 13+I which suffered engine failure near Vannes on 4 February 1943 and the unknown pilot was forced to bale out but landed uninjured. Note the eagle's head has now been applied forward of the exhausts.

Otto Kleinert at readiness on his A-3's port main wheel, Cherbourg, summer 1942.

When Gruppen Kommandeur of III./Jagdgeschwader 2, Hauptmann Hans Hahn flew Fw 190 A-3, *werk nummer* 223, and by the time he handed over to Oberleutnant Egon Mayer, he had sixty-five kills. Mayer's score at the time he took over command was fifty-two kills. However, this aircraft appears to have sixty-eight kills on its rudder – Mayer's 68th kill did not come until 14 July 1943 by which time he was Kommodore of Jagdgeschwader 2.

Otto Kleinert on the award of the Eiserne Kreuz Second Class, Vannes, March 1943. The Fw 190 A-3 behind is unusual as initially it is thought it had tropical filters for operations in North Africa. However, in September 1942, the lightweight Fw 190 A-3/U7 was produced with a BMW 801 C engine, carburettor air intakes outside and fuselage guns removed. Werk nummer 528, 530 and 531 were then to be used as a high-altitude Höhenjäger.

Opposite: Leutnant Friedrich Fleischmann in front of what is believed to be an Fw 190 A-3/U7. Clipped to the oral inflation tube of his 10-30 life preserver is a wrist compass and he appears to be carrying a victory stick.

Another possible A-3/U7 seen with 9./Jagdgeschwader 2.

Opposite: The rudder of 'Assi' Hahn's Fw 190 A-3; he is in the white jacket second from the right. Sixty-one kills on the rudder would date this photo as being taken between 6 May and 6 June 1942.

Otto Kleinert beneath an A-2/A-3 undergoing work at Cherbourg, summer 1942.

Leutnant Kurt Bühligen scored his first kill over England on 9 September 1940 as an Unteroffizier with 4./Jagdgeschwader 2. He would be awarded the Ritterkreuz on 4 September 1941 as an Oberfeldwebel but was promoted to Leutnant shortly afterwards. He then took command of 4./Jagdgeschwader 2 at the start of August 1942 and in November 1942, his Gruppe moved to Tunisia.

Oberleutnant Josef Wurmheller started the war as an NCO with 2./Jagdgeschwader 53, then moving to 5./Jagdgeschwader 53 before joining II./Jagdgeschwader 2 in the summer of 1941. His first kill with Jagdgeschwader 2 came on 24 July 1941 and he was awarded the Ritterkreuz on 4 September 1941. The rudder of his Fw 190 A-5 shows seventy-four kills, the most recent being a B-17 on 4 July 1943 by which time he had been awarded the Eichenlaub on 13 November 1942 and having been promoted to Leutnant the previous month. (via Kerstner)

Josef Wurmheller alongside his Fw 190, presumed to be A-5 werk nummer 2648.

Opposite: Wurmheller's 78th kill was a Spitfire on 16 August 1943. This Fw 190 A-6 werk nummer 530314 coded Yellow 2 of 9./Jagdgeschwader 2 was destroyed after being hit by bombs at Vannes on 23 September 1943; Wurmheller was also wounded. (via Kerstner)

Opposite: A-4 werk nummer 0746 showing Schnell's seventy-five kills. This aircraft ended its days as Blue 25 with training unit 4./Jagdgeschwader 101 and at 0917hrs on 1 October 1944, it crashed at Fuchshain, killing its pilot Fahnenjunker-Unteroffizier Rudolf Schramm

Fw 190 A-4 werk nummer 746 coded Yellow 4+I flown by Oberleutnant Siegfried Schnell, Staffelkapitän of 9./Jagdgeschwader 2. He would hand over command to Josef Wurmheller at the start of April 1943 by which time his score stood at seventy-five. He too had started the war as an NCO and had been awarded the Ritterkreuz and Eichenlaub.

Wurmheller's seventy-three kills would date this photograph as between 28 June and 4 July 1943. Werk nummer 2648 and coded Yellow 2+I.

Wurmheller in the cockpit of his Fw 190; he would be killed in action over Normandy on 22 June 1944 in an Fw 190 A-8 werk nummer 171053 whilst commanding III./Jagdgeschwader 2; his final score was 102.

Opposite: Werk nummer 281 (in full, 5281) identifies this as an Fw 190 A-2 and the kill tally that of Oberleutnant Siegfried Schnell, Staffelkapitän of 9./Jagdgeschwader 2. The top shows forty kills and the fact that he had been awarded the Ritterkreuz (9 November 1940) and Eichenlaub (9 July 1941). The rudder shows sixty-two kills (the 62nd being on 4 June 1942) and it is not certain if more are being added as sixty-three and sixty-four came on 6 June 1942 and the 65th not until 26 June 1942. Schnell would be killed in action flying a Bf 109 G-6 whilst commanding IV./Jagdgeschwader 54; his final score stood at ninety-three.

An unidentified pilot of 9./Jagdgeschwader 2 in an Fw 190 A. On the cowling in front of him are his flare cartridges. The only record of a Yellow 11 was an Fw 190 A-5 werk nummer 1199 which suffered 20 per cent damage in an accident at Vannes on 1 May 1943.

On 30 January 1944, Flying Officer Charles Demoulin of 609 Squadron was credited with the destruction of two Fw 190s in the Gisors/Roye area of France at around 1310hrs. This camera-gun shot shows an Fw 190 A trying to get away from Demoulin but to no avail. Jagdgeschwader 2 lost a number of aircraft in that area around that time. Hauptmann Bernhard Schenkbier, Staffelkapitän of 10./Jagdgeschwader 2, was killed when his Fw 190 A-4 werk nummer 470036 was shot down near Beaumont/Oise at 1250hrs. Leutnant Willi Linnhoff of 9./Jagdgeschwader 2 was killed in the same area in an Fw 190 A-6 werk nummer 530902 at 1300hrs, as was Unteroffizier Otto Fischer of 11./Jagdgeschwader 2, who was killed flying Fw 190 A-6 werk nummer 551122 at 1250hrs. Finally Hauptmann Fritz Edelmann Geschwader, Adjutant of Jagdgeschwader 2, was shot down and killed 10km north-east of Senlis in an Fw 190 A-7/R6 werk nummer 430473. It should be stated that 198 Squadron also claimed nine Fw 190s destroyed, one probable and two damaged in the Rouen/Laroche area. German records state they were attacked by P-47s but all P-47 claims were either over Germany, Belgium or Holland.

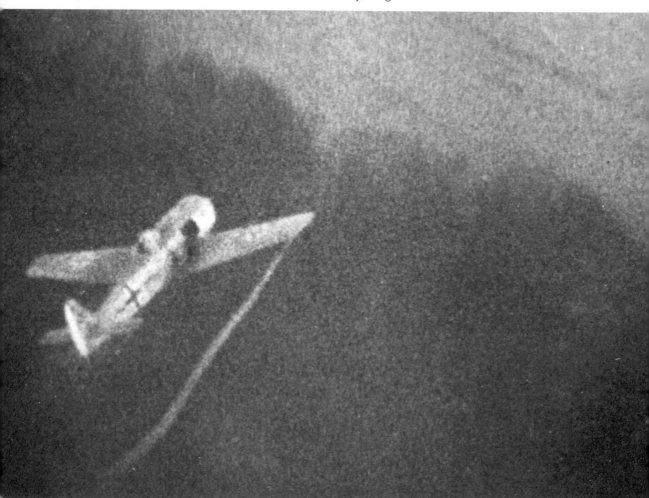

At 1515hrs on 17 March 1944, Fw 190 A-6 werk nummer 551097 was attacked by Allied fighters whilst taking off from Chartres and its pilot, Fähnrich Heinz Liebick of 9./Jagdgeschwader 2, was wounded. Chartres was attacked by 361st Fighter Group that afternoon. Fifteen P-47s of the 374th Fighter Squadron remained at altitude acting as top cover while the 375th and 376th Fighter Squadrons carried out the low-level attack. Two enemy aircraft were claimed destroyed on the ground (a Bf 109 and one unidentified) along with four damaged (a Ju 88, two Bf 109s and one unidentified). Major George Merritt spotted a taxiing Bf 109 which he hit repeatedly, bringing it to violent halt. According to Merritt's combat report, 'after passing over, I observed the [enemy aircraft] ground looping to the left, and the landing gear collapsing as the plane was enveloped in a cloud of dust and smoke'. It is believed that the aircraft claimed by Major Merritt was Liebick's Fw 190. This photo shows Liebick after his recovery and having been promoted to Leutnant. It is believed he had two claims on 5 and 11 July 1944.

OTHER JAGDGESCHWADER IN NORTH-WEST EUROPE

With his back to the camera is Hauptmann Peter-Paul Stendl of 1./Jagdgeschwader 26. To the far right is Hauptmann Joahnnes Seifert whose first kill was on 10 May 1940 with 3./Jagdgeschwader 26. He then commanded I./Jagdgeschwader 26 where this photo was taken, was awarded the Ritterkreuz on 7 June 1942 but was killed in action commanding II./Jagdgeschwader 26 on 25 November 1943 when his Fw 190 A-6, werk nummer 470006 Black double chevron, crashed at La Couture near Bethune. His 57th kill, a P-38 of the 343rd Fighter Squadron 55th Fighter Group flown by Lieutenant Manuel Aldecoa, came at the same time as their aircraft are believed to have collided.

Opposite: Fw 190 A-1, werk nummer 033 of 6./Jagdgeschwader 26 coded Black 6. This was one of five aircraft lost in accidents on the afternoon of 22 December 1941. Whilst moving from Wevelghem in Belgium to Abbeville-Drucat in France, 6./Jagdgeschwader 26 led by Oberleutnant Walter Schneider (who had twenty kills to his name) got lost in fog and the pilots became disorientated. Five aircraft crashed with all five pilots, including Schneider, being killed. The pilot of this aircraft was former infantryman Oberfeldwebel Kurt Görbig who had joined 6./Jagdgeschwader 26 at the end of August 1941 direct from training. He was killed when the aircraft crashed at Echingen, 4km south-east of Boulogne. (via Price)

An Fw 190 A-3 of 6./Jagdgeschwader 26 taken in the summer of 1942 at Abbeville-Drucat. In December 1942, 6./Jagdgeschwader 26 began to convert to the Bf 109 G-4.

Opposite: A well-known series of photographs of an Fw 190 being attacked by Flight Sergeant Tony Robson of 485 Squadron near Ambleteuse on the evening of 4 May 1942. Robson reported 'Flying as Blue 2 at 17,000 feet, I saw two Fw 190s 2,000 feet below. Blue 12 dived to attack and I followed him. I fired two short bursts at one. He turned inland and I followed him to close range and fired the rest of my ammunition at him. I saw several hits. One wheel came down, the hood and pilot's helmet blew off. The enemy aircraft when last seen was flying with the starboard wing down at about 2,000 feet.' Blue 1, Flight Lieutenant Mick Shand, also claimed an Fw 190 probable at 1945hrs but no losses can be matched. However, an Fw 190 A-2, werk nummer 5260 Black 2 of 2./Jagdgeschwader 26, crash-landed at St Omer-Arques with 25 per cent damage. Flying Officer A. R. Robson would be the pilot of one of three 485 Squadron Spitfires shot down by Hauptmann Wilhelm-Ferdinand Galland of II./Jagdgeschwader 26, Leutnant Helmut Hoppe of 5./Jagdgeschwader 26 and Oberleutnant Johannes Naumann of 6./Jagdgeschwader 26 around midday on 13 February 1943. He was taken prisoner whilst the other two pilots were killed. Flight Lieutenant Mick Shand would be awarded the DFC but would be shot down together with another Spitfire from 485 Squadron around midday on 28 November 1942 by Unteroffizier Fuchs and Feldwebel Ernst Winkler of 4./Jagdgeschwader 1. He was taken prisoner but the other pilot was killed.

Hauptmann Paul Steindl (right) talking with (to his right) Unteroffizier Karl 'Charly' Willius of 3./Jagdgeschwader 26 and an unidentified pilot. Steindl first flew with Stab II./Jagdgeschwader 54 before being posted to be Staffelkapitän of 4. (Einsätz)/Jagdfliegerschule 4 and then joining Stab./Jagdgeschwader 26 at the end of 1941. Promoted to Hauptmann in April 1942, he was then with 1./Jagdgeschwader 26 before he was posted in November 1942 to be Staffelkapitän of 5./Jagdgeschwader 54. In April 1943, he returned to I./Jagdgeschwader 26, took temporary command of 9./Jagdgeschwader 26 and in June 1943 took command of 11./Jagdgeschwader 26 until January 1944 when he returned to Stab I./Jagdgeschwader 26. His first kill was on 11 October 1942 with 1./Jagdgeschwader 26. He then had six kills with 5./Jagdgeschwader 54 and another two with 9 and 11./Jagdgeschwader 26. He would be wounded in action on 3 November 1943 flying a Bf 109 G-6 but would be killed in an accident on 9 January 1945 flying an Fw 190 D-9 werk nummer 210983 Black 10 with Stab./Jagdgeschwader 2. Willius came to 3./Jagdgeschwader 26 in August 1941 from Jagdgeschwader 51 and shot down a total of fifty aircraft. His last was a B-24 on 8 April 1944 by which time he was leading 2./Jagdgeschwader 26. He was shot down by a P-47 of the 361st Fighter Group and his Fw 190 A-8, werk nummer 170009 Black 4, crashed near Zwolle-Kamperzeedijk. Note the 3./Jagdgeschwader 26 Fw 190 Yellow 5 in the background.

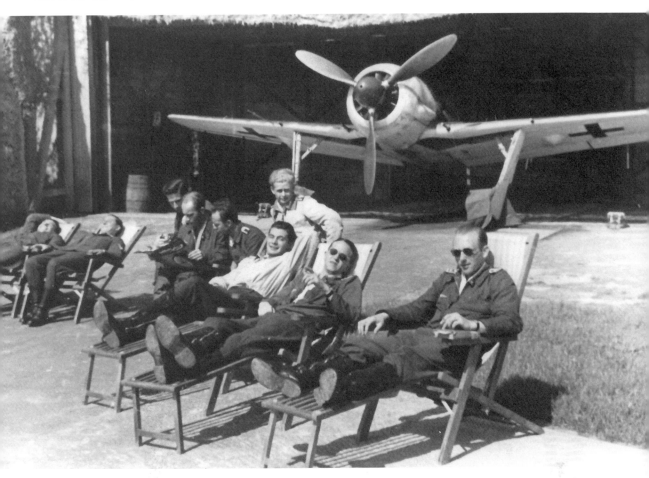

6./Jagdgeschwader 26 at readiness in front of one of their Fw 190 A-3s, Abbeville-Drucat, July 1942. Left to right: Leutnant Rudolf Leuschel (+ 25 February 1944 with 8./Jagdgeschwader 26), Gefreiter Friedrich Kaiser (+ 16 May 1942), Unteroffizier Heinz Budde (POW 20 January 1943), Unteroffizier Wilhelm Mayer (Ritterkreuz, + with 8./Jagdgeschwader 26 4 January 1945), ?, Unteroffizier Heinz Marquardt (POW 20 January 1943), Leutnant Robert Weiss (Ritterkreuz and Eichenlaub, + III./Jagdgeschwader 54 29 December 1944), Leutnant Walter Matoni (Ritterkreuz), Oberfeldwebel Kurt Kruska (+ 9 April 1943).

A view of an Fw 190 A-4 of III./Jagdgeschwader 26 in its purpose-built hangar, Wevelghem, 1942.

Opposite above: Major Gerhard Schöpfel (centre) commanded III./Jagdgeschwader 26 from August 1940 to December 1941 when he took over Jagdgeschwader 26; in both cases he took over from Adolf Galland. He would be awarded the Ritterkreuz in September 1940 and would shoot down a total of forty-five aircraft, all with Jagdgeschwader 26. To the left is Hauptmann Johannes Seifert, Gruppen Kommandeur of I./Jagdgeschwader 26.

Opposite below: The same aircraft from a slightly different angle showing the low camouflaged roof and how the aircraft fits in perfectly.

FOCKE-WULF FW 190   OTHER JAGDGESCHWADER IN NORTH-WEST EUROPE

Believed to be Feldwebel Adolf Glunz returning from a mission. His first kill was with 4./Jagdgeschwader 52 on 7 May 1941. By August 1941, his score stood at six by which time he was flying with 4./Jagdgeschwader 26 on the Channel coast. His 20th kill came on 31 July 1942 but he was most successful in 1943 by the end of which he had shot down fifty-one aircraft. He would survive the war with seventy-one kills.

Opposite above: Mechanics working on a III./Jagdgeschwader 26 aircraft at Wevelghem, late 1942.

Opposite below: Pilots of 6./Jagdgeschwader 26 recounting a combat at Abbeville-Drucat, September 1942. Left to right: Oberfeldwebel Kurt Kruska, Leutnant Rolf Leuschel, Leutnant Walter Matoni, Leutnant Helmut Hoppe (+ 1 December 1943 with 5./Jagdgeschwader 26), Oberfeldwebel Adolf Glunz (4./Jagdgeschwader 26, Ritterkreuz & Eichenlaub), and Unteroffizier Heinz Marquardt.

83

Opposite above: Final photo for 6./Jagdgeschwader, 26 September 1942. Left to right: Unteroffizier Heinz Budde, Unteroffizier Heinz Marquardt, Unteroffizier Gerhard Vogt, Oberleutnant Theo Lindemann, Leutnant Heinz Hoppe, Leutnant Rolf Leuschel, Leutnant Kurt-Erich Wenzel (+ 20 January 1943), and Unteroffizier Wilhelm Mayer.

Opposite below: An Fw 190 A-5 werk nummer 1197 White 1 of 4./Jagdgeschwader 26, 1943. White 1 was given to A-4 werk nummer 2405 and A-6 werk nummer 530727 in 1943 so it is assumed this aircraft was photographed between May and November 1943. 4./Jagdgeschwader 26 was commanded by Hauptmann Helmut Hoppe during this period.

Saying goodbye to the Staffelkapitän of 6./Jagdgeschwader 26, Abbeville-Drucat September 1942. Left to right: Unteroffizier Heinz Budde, Unteroffizier Heinz Marquart, Oberleutnant Johannes Naumann (new Staffelkapitän, Ritterkreuz), Unteroffizier Gerhard Vogt (hidden – Ritterkreuz, + 14 January 1945 with 5./Jagdgeschwader 26), Oberleutnant Theo Lindemann (outgoing Staffelkapitän), Leutnant Rolf Leuschel, Leutnant Heinz Hoppe, and Unteroffizier Wilhelm Mayer

Photographed at Wevelghem on 3 January 1943 is Unteroffizier Robert Hager of 8./Jagdgeschwader 26 with his mechanic. Seventeen days later he was injured in an accident landing at Calais Marck after a combat mission in his Fw 190 A-4, werk nummer 7102 Black 4, possibly this aircraft. On 4 April 1943, he was credited with a Spitfire but at the same time was wounded flying an Fw 190 A-4, werk nummer 2391 Black 11. He then appears to move to 4./Jagdgeschwader 26 with which he shot down another three aircraft. However, he was killed in action on 13 August 1944 when his Fw 190 A-8, werk nummer 172674 Green 3, was shot down near Le Mans.

Photographed at Boissy-le-Bois in June–July 1944 is Leutnant Georg Kiefner of 1./Jagdgeschwader 26 together with his mechanic. Behind is Fw 190 A-8, werk nummer 171079 White 5, which was shot down by American anti-aircraft fire between Chartres and Alencon. Kiefner would be credited with twelve aircraft but was shot down or wounded five times. He survived the war.

The background would appear Scandinavian and the Fw 190 A-2 nearest the camera has the werk nummer 318 and six kill markings. Werk nummer 0318 of IV./Jagdgeschwader 5 was reported overturning on take-off from Gossen in Norway on 11 December 1943 and suffering 25 per cent damage. It is possible that it was then modified to an A-3 as on 10 April 1944 werk nummer 0318 of 10./Jagdgeschwader 5 crashed in the sea and its pilot, Feldwebel Kurt Drössler, baled out but was killed. Drössler had four kills by the time of his death and is still listed as missing.

Opposite: Unteroffizier Albert Meyer was one of three pilots of II./Jagdgeschwader 26 to be killed on the afternoon of 3 April 1943. Scrambled from Vitry to intercept Typhoons attacking Abbeville-Drucat, they were bounced by Spitfires of the Kenley Wing lead by Wing Commander Johnny Johnson. 403 Squadron claimed to have destroyed three Fw 190s near Fruges, and 416 Squadron claimed to have destroyed two Fw 190s near Le Touquet and damaged another, whilst Johnny Johnson claimed an Fw 190 destroyed east of Montrueil. Unteroffizier Hans Heiss' Fw 190 A-4, werk nummer 2440 Brown 5 of 6./Jagdgeschwader 26 crashed at Neuville near to Montrueil which matches well with Johnson's claim. Unteroffizier Heinrich Damm's Fw 190 A-4, werk nummer 732 White 11 of 4./Jagdgeschwader 26, crashed at La Paix Faite, 9km south-east of Etaples a possible victim of Flight Lieutenant Bob Buckham and Flying Officer Norman Keene of 416 Squadron. As for Unteroffizier Albert Meyer, he and his Fw 190 A-5, werk nummer 1159 Black 5 of 5./Jagdgeschwader 26, disappeared. It is possible that he was a victim of Squadron Leader Foss Boulton of 416 Squadron whose victim exploded off the coast.

The back of this photo is inscribed 'Spitfire', 'Jagdgeschwader 5' and 'Herdla'. The only possibility is 27 September 1942 when Gefreiter Kurt Dobner of 11./Jagdgeschwader 5 shot down a Spitfire at 1129hrs. On this day Spitfire BP889 of 1 Photographic Reconnaissance Unit was lost over Norway, crashing at Lavselv and killing the pilot, Pilot Officer G. W. Walker. On 5 April 1943, Dobner, now flying with 14 (Jabo)./Jagdgeschwader 5 was shot down by Flak in Fw 190 A-3, werk nummer 130323 Black 14, west of Murmaschi. The successful pilot (left) is being congratulated by an administrative officer, identifiable by his rank tabs.

Believed photographed at Rheine is this Fw 190 A-5, werk nummer 2700 Black 8, of I./Jagdgeschwader 11. An aircraft with this werk nummer suffered a technical problem and had to make a forced landing at Friedrichstadt on 12 August 1943. 'Rübezahl' was a fairytale giant/mountain troll said to live in the Riesengebirge, a mountain range in Silesia, so perhaps the regular pilot came from that region.

An Fw 190 tries desperately to get away from the guns of a P-47 flown by Captain Walter Beckham of the 351st Fighter Squadron. Beckham was credited with the destruction of this aircraft near Dülmen at 1415 hrs on 11 November 1943. I./Jagdgeschwader 1 lost four Fw 190s that afternoon. However, a possibility is an Fw 190 A-6, werk nummer 550803 Black 4 of 5./Jagdgeschwader 1, was reported to have been shot down by a P-47 and crashed at Limbergen, north-east of Dülmen, its pilot Unteroffizier Erwin Wessely being killed.

Opposite: The full werk nummer of this Fw 190 A-5 is 410055 of 1./Jagdgeschwader 1 which force-landed at Speyerdorf on 17 August 1943 after combat. It again suffered a technical problem on 18 October 1943 still with 1./Jagdgeschwader 1 and force-landed at Deelen suffering 65 per cent damage and its pilot, Oberfeldwebel Fritz Bahl, was injured. The pilot in this photo is believed to be Unteroffizier Bernhard Kunze of 1./Jagdgeschwader 1 whose first kill was a B-17 on 13 June 1943. He got his fourth on 17 August 1943 (another B-17) and his fifth (yet another B-17) was two days later. By the end of 1943 he had been credited with seven B-17s, a P-47 and a B-24. However, on 5 January 1944 and now with 2./Jagdgeschwader 1, Feldwebel Kunze's Fw 190 A-6, werk nummer 550884 Black 6, was damaged in combat and crashed at Bergisch-Gladbach, killing the pilot. Kunze would receive the Ehrenpokal posthumously on 17 April 1944.

In 1944 a number of Fw 190s from Jagdgeschwader 26 were found abandoned on Melsbroek airfield in Belgium. This is Fw 190 A-8, werk nummer 175140 Blue 6+- of 8./Jagdgeschwader 26.

Opposite: Werk nummer 550476 was an Fw 190 A-6 and with sixteen kills is the mount of an ace. Oberfeldwebel Georg 'Murr' Schott had flown in Spain with the Legion Condor shooting down three aircraft. He then had twelve kills with I.(Jagd)/Lehrgeschwader 2 by the end of the Battle of Britain. He would get his 13th on 10 January 1941. In April 1942, he arrived at 10./Jagdgeschwader 1 and once commissioned took command of 1./Jagdgeschwader 1 in June 1943. His first kill was a B-17 on 22 June and he had another two claims after that. It would appear that his kill being marked here is his 16th, a B-17 on 28 July 1943. On 27 September 1943 he was shot down by P-47s in this aircraft coded White 11 (P-47s of the 67th Fighter Squadron claimed three Fw 190s near Borkum or south of Juist). He was seen to bale out and get into his dinghy but the dinghy with his dead body in it was washed ashore on the island of Sylt on 11 October 1943.

Another view of Blue 6+-. At this time, 8./Jagdgeschwader 26 was commanded by Ritterkreuz winner Leutnant Heinz Kemethmüller and is not reported to have been based at Melsbroeck. Even though the RAF pilots did not know it, this wreck had apparently been booby-trapped.

Opposite above: Fw 190 A-8, werk nummer 171568 White 7+- of 5./Jagdgeschwader 26. At the end of August 1944, 5./Jagdgeschwader 26 was commanded by Hauptmann Georg-Peter Eder who handed over to Oberleutnant Adolf Glunz on moving to Germany. Both had received the Ritterkreuz: Eder would receive the Eichenlaub in November 1944 whilst Glunz had been awarded the Eichenlaub in June 1944.

Opposite below: Nose-on view of White 7 showing clearly the spiral spinner. II./Jagdgeschwader 26 moved to Meslbroek on 29 August 1944 but five days later moved back to Germany

JABO

An Fw 190 A-5/U8 of 10 (Jabo)./Jagdgeschwader 26 at St Omer-Wizernes, early 1943.
10./Jagdgeschwader 26 used a mix of A-2s, A-3s and A-4s but by March 1943 was operating
A-5s. In February 1943 it became 10./Jagdgeschwader 54 and at the end of March formed
IV./Schnellkampfgeschwader 10.

Two Fw 190 A-4s/A-5s of 10./Jagdgeschwader 26 taxying out at St Omer-Wizernes for a mission, each carrying a single 250kg bomb. Just visible is the latter part of the unit badge which would be a black numeral, then a cross, then a single black chevron followed by a stylized black bomb with white fins.

An Fw 190 A-5/U8 of an unidentified unit. It has a single 250kg bomb and two 300-litre (966 imperial gallon) drop tanks.

Aircrew and groundcrew having a closer look at Wenger's plane, Théville, 10 January 1943. At far left is Heinz Schumann and third from left is Unteroffizier Kurt Bressler who would be shot down and killed by 266 Squadron off Exmouth on 26 February 1943 while flying Fw 190 A-5 werk nummer 2588. In the middle is Leopold Wenger.

Opposite above: A 250kg bomb about to be loaded on Fw 190 A-2, werk nummer 081 Blue 3+<-, of 10./Jagdgeschwader 2, Caen-Carpiquet, late 1942.

Opposite below: Leutnant Leopold Wenger inspects damage to his Fw 190 A-4 Blue 13+<-, Théville, 10 January 1943. The damage occurred attacking Teignmouth and was either caused by anti-aircraft fire or Flying Officer Sam Blackwell of 266 Squadron who reporting damaging an Fw 190 in the wing. To the right is the new Staffelkapitän, Hauptmann Heinz Schumann. Both pilots would be awarded the Ritterkreuz, Wenger being killed in action 10 April 1945 and Schumann in an accident on 8 November 1943.

Opposite above: Close-up of the damage to Storsberg's Fw 190.

Opposite below: The entrance hole on the starboard side of Storsberg's aircraft.

Oberleutnant Siegfried Storsberg of 10./Jagdgeschwader 26 standing alongside his Fw 190 A-4/A-5, early 1943. Behind him is the chevron and stylized bomb. The numeral would either be Black 1 or 11 – Black 1 was an A-4 werk nummer 2435 and shot down off Beachy Head by 609 Squadron on 5 February 1943, killing Unteroffizier Herbert Büttner, whilst Black 11 was an A-5 werk nummer 0835 shot down by anti-aircraft fire off Eastbourne on 3 April 1943 killing Unteroffizier Fritz Ebert.

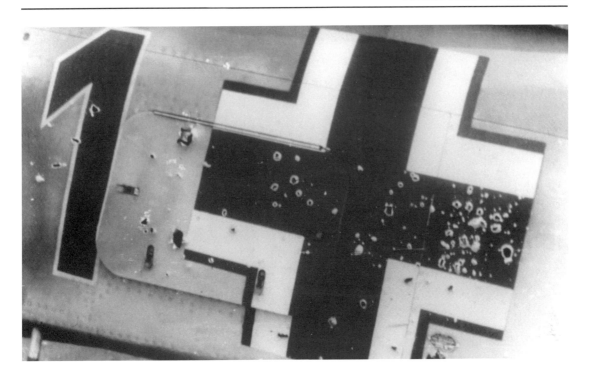

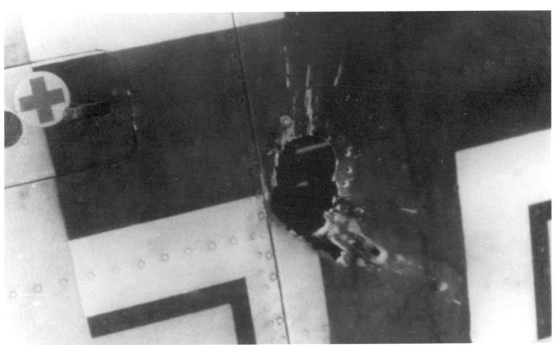

It takes four men to load a drop tank: 2./Schnellkampfgeschwader 10, summer 1943.

Opposite above: Loading a 250kg bomb on an Fw 190 G-3 Jabo, Western Front 1944. In August 1944 I./Schnellkampfgeschwader 10 became III./Kampfgeschwader 51 and in November 1944 Nachtschlachtgruppe 20.

Opposite below: Note it also takes four men to load a 250kg bomb.

Opposite above: An Fw 190 A-4/A-5 of 10./Jagdgeschwader 26 in its hangar either at Wevelghem or St Omer-Wizernes, 1942–3.

Opposite below: Leutnant Leopold Wenger's Fw 190 A-2 Blue 12+<-, photographed at Caen-Carpiquet, 24 February 1943.

The rear fuselage of Oberfeldwebel Werner Kassa's Fw 190 A-2, *werk nummer* 2080 Black 13, of 10./Jagdgeschwader 26. This aircraft was shot down by light anti-aircraft fire and crashed inverted at Lottbridge Drove, Eastbourne at 0934hrs on 26 August 1942. The pilot was obviously killed.

Opposite above: By the end of March 1943, II./Schnellkampfgeschwader 10 was almost ready to be committed to operations. This photo was taken at Caen-Carpiquet on 25 March 1943 and shows (left to right) Hauptmann Hans Curt Graf von Sponeck, Staffelkapitän of 5./Schnellkampfgeschwader 10, Major Günther Tonne Geschwader Kommodore (+ 15 July 1943), Hauptmann Karl-Friedrich Böttger (Gruppen Ia II./Schnellkampfgeschwader 10) and Leutnant Fritz Setzer of 5./Schnellkampfgeschwader 10 (POW 17 April 1943). In the background is an Fw 190 A-5 with the Schnellkampfgeschwader 10 triangle ahead of the cross and the letter White C or G of 5 Staffel.

Opposite below: Hauptmann Hans Curt Graf von Sponeck serves the champagne celebrating the award of the Eiserne Kreuz to a number of II./Schnellkampfgeschwader 10 pilots. Von Sponeck was an experienced fighter pilot, having flown with Jagdgeschwader 131 and 132 before the war and then Jagdgeschwader 2 at the start of the war. By the end of 1940, he was with II./Jagdgeschwader 54 but from February 1941 commanded 10./Jagdgeschwader 3 which soon became 1.(Einsatz) Ergänzungs Jagdgruppe/Jagdgeschwader 3. In January 1942 he took command of 7./Jagdgeschwader 5 where he got two kills – 23 April and 15 May 1942. In 1943, he took command of 5./Schnellkampfgeschwader 10. He did very little operational flying and from August 1943 onwards held a series of Staff appointments.

Oberleutnant Paul 'Bomben' Keller, Staffelkapitän of 10./Jagdgeschwader 26 and ultimately 10./Jagdgeschwader 54. He was awarded the Deutsches Kreuz in Gold at the end of November 1942 but was then killed attacking Ashford in Kent on 24 March 1943. His Fw 190 A-5, werk nummer 2587 Black 7+<-, exploded when light anti-aircraft fire hit the bomb he was carrying. He was killed instantly.

An Fw 190 A-5 of 2./Schnellkampfgeschwader 10, summer 1943.

Opposite above: Having carried out a number of operational flights with 10./Jagdgeschwader 26, in the autumn of 1942 Unteroffizier Richard Wittmann was posted to Erprobungs-und-Lehrkommando 22 at Rechlin-Lärz for development of the long-range Jabos (Jagdbomber mit vergrösserter Reichweite, or Jaborei). The cause of this crash-landing or its date is not known.

Opposite below: An Fw 190 A of I./Schnellkampfgeschwader 10 getting airborne from Dreux on a non-operational flight. Note the drop tank as opposed to a bomb under the fuselage.

When 10./Jagdgeschwader 2 became 13./Schnellkampfgeschwader 10 in March/April 1943, aircraft numerals were replaced by letters. Blue 12, favoured by Oberleutnant Leopold Wenger who now commanded 13./Schnellkampfgeschwader 10, became Blue E but retained the Blue 12 on the cowling.

Opposite above: An Fw 190 A-3 of 10./Schnellkampfgeschwader 10 coded Blue 12+<-, flown by Leutnant Leopold Wenger, having suffered a partial undercarriage collapse at Ste André, 31 July 1942. Note the 10./Jagdgeschwader 2 fox-with-a-ship badge.

Opposite below: The 10./Jagdgeschwader 2 badge was a russet fox carrying a grey-blue ship. It is not known whether this badge was carried on IV./Schnellkampfgeschwader 10 aircraft when 10./Jagdgeschwader 2 and 10./Jagdgeschwader 54 went to form this Gruppe. In October 1943, IV./Schnellkampfgeschwader 10 became II./Schlachtgeschwader 10 and operated on the Eastern Front where this badge was adopted, a Soviet star being added to the right of the ship.

Opposite above: Oberleutnant Leopold Wenger climbing out of his Fw 190 A-5 Blue 12 at Caen-Carpiquet, spring 1943. The fact that the aircraft has numerals as opposed to letters is proof it was still 10./Jagdgeschwader 2 not 13./Schnellkampfgeschwader 10.

Opposite below: In response to the Allied landings in North Africa on 8 November 1942, 10./Jagdgeschwader 2 and 10./Jagdgeschwader 26 were rushed to Marseilles-Istres in southern France. No operational flights were flown and both Staffel returned north in mid-December 1942. This photograph shows 10./Jagdgeschwader 2 at Istres on 29 November 1943. The nearest aircraft is coded Blue 11 – Fw 190 A-5, werk nummer 1106 coded Blue 11, was shot down by 486 Squadron off Bognor Regis on 1 March 1943 killing Unteroffizier Ernst Läpple. However, at the time this photo was taken, 10./Jagdgeschwader 2 was still flying the A-3 variant.

Leutnant Otto-August Backhaus and an unidentified Oberfeldwebel of 10./Jagdgeschwader 54. In the background is one of the Staffel's Fw 190 A-5s at St Omer-Wizernes. Backhaus was shot down by a Typhoon of 609 Squadron on the evening of 9 April 1943 flying Fw 190 A-5 Black 12 whilst searching for Unteroffizier Karl Heck who had been shot down by anti-aircraft fire earlier in the day flying Fw 190 A-05, *werk nummer* 0831 Black 14. Both pilots were killed.

Staffelkapitän Leopold Wenger is third from left and to his right is Feldwebel Walter 'Pipifax' Peiler who would be killed with 4./Schlachtgeschwader 10 (formerly 13./Schnellkampfgeschwader 10), on 1 June 1944.

Opposite above: Oberleutnant Leopold Wenger's A-5 Blue 12/E of 13./Schnellkampfgeschwader 10 seen at Caen-Carpiquet, 26 May 1943. Note how the camouflage has changed from the clean camouflage of the aircraft at Istres in November 1942.

Opposite below: Pilots of 13./Schnellkampfgeschwader 10, late May 1943. Sitting on the wheel is Leopold Wenger and to his right is who is believed to be Leutnant Hermann Müller. Note what appears to be an A-5 with the letter A – 13 Staffel had blue letters, 14 Staffel black letters and 15 Staffel yellow letters.

The first attempt to use the Fw 190 as a night Jabo on 16/17 April 1943 was a disaster. I./Schnellkampfgeschwader 10 lost one aircraft on operations with six in accidents with three pilots killed and one injured, whilst II Gruppe lost four aircraft and one damaged with three pilots captured and one killed. This is Fw 190 A-4, werk nummer 7155 Yellow H, of 7./Schnellkampfgeschwader 10, whose pilot, Feldwebel Otto Bechtold, landed at RAF West Malling in Kent. A second aircraft crashed on the approach to West Malling and a final aircraft landed on fire and was burnt out. Note the hastily-applied black distemper. The camouflage was described as Yellow H outlined in black, triangle in black, last three digits of werk nummer on the fin. Upper surface was in two or three different shades of grey but the fuselage was mottled blue-gray. The underside of the engine cowling and rudder were yellow but the whole aircraft was smeared with what was described as a 'oil-lamp black mixture'. The spinner was green, yellow and white with the white smeared with lamp black.

Opposite above: Believed to be the last moments of Fw 190 A-5, *werk nummer* 1412 Blue F, of 13./Schnellkampfgeschwader 10 which was shot down by Flight Sergeant Brian Calnan of 257 Squadron after attacking Torquay in the afternoon of 30 May 1943. The Jabo is reported to have crashed on Alderney in the Channel Islands, killing Leutnant Hermann Müller whose body was never recovered.

Opposite below: Feldwebel Richard Wittmann of 2./Schnellkampfgeschwader 10 and his Fw 190 A-5. I./Schnellkampfgeschwader 10 was used for night attacks over the UK and then the Normandy beaches from April 1943. It would become III./Kampfgeschwader 51 in August 1944. Wittmann would be awarded the Deutsches Kreuz in Gold in February 1945 by which time his unit had become 2./Nachtschlachtgruppe 20.

Opposite above: Both drop tanks had been jettisoned after crossing the Kent coast.

Opposite below: The aircraft was flown to the Royal Aircraft Establishment, being assigned the serial PE822. It was then delivered to 1426 (Enemy Aircraft) Flight at RAF Collyweston. It caught fire in the air on 13 October 1944and then crashed on the Stamford to Kettering road killed the Flight's commanding officer, Flight Lieutenant Ernest Lewendon.

Outside the watch office at West Malling with instructions to all to keep off! The temporary nature of the lamp-black camouflage is clear.

Klahn's aircraft dived into the ground at Staplehurst in Kent at high speed, disintegrated and caught fire. This is what was left of one of the wings and undercarriage; in the background is the engine.

Opposite: Oberleutnant Hans Klahn Staffelkapitän of 2./Schnellkampfgeschwader 10 was an experienced pilot. He was shot down and taken prisoner over France on 18 May 1940 whilst with 6./Kampfgeschwader 55. Released after the French surrender, he joined I./Kampfgeschwader 40, flying the Fw 200, on 13 January 1941, remaining with that unit until June 1942 by which time he had been awarded the Ehrenpokal. He now joined Erprobungs und Lehrstaffel He 177 but in December 1942, joined I./Schnellkampfgeschwader 10. On the night of 16 April 1943, it is believed he became lost or disorientated attacking London. He baled out too low from his Fw 190 A-5 werk nummer 2697 and was killed.

Another loss on 23 May 1943 was Unteroffizier Eugen Streich of 15./Schnellkampfgeschwader 10, but he was killed in a training flight.

Opposite above: The remains of the other wing from Klahn's Fw 190 A-5.

Opposite below: The remains of Fw 190 A-5, werk nummer 50136 Yellow H, of 15./Schnellkampfgeschwader 10. Hit by anti-aircraft fire in a daylight Jabo attack on Bournemouth on 23 May 1943, it crashed into a house at 34 Grove Road before Unteroffizier Friedrich-Karl Schmidt could release the 500kg bomb it was carrying. Schmidt was killed and the bomb later exploded. Some records say this aircraft was White H as opposed to Yellow H.

An earlier Jabo loss over land occurred on 20 January 1943. During a massed daylight attack on London, Leutnant Hermann Hoch flying in Fw 190 A-4, werk nummer 2409 Black 2+<-, of 10./Jagdgeschwader 26, was hit by anti-aircraft fire and tried to land near Capel only for his aircraft to hit the top of a hill, bounce 200 yards and plough through a coppice. The engine broke away and the aircraft somersaulted, but Hoch escaped serious injury, put his papers and parachute in the cockpit and initiated the demolition charge which effectively destroyed what was left of the engine. This photograph shows the rear fuselage (the 10./Jagdgeschwader 26 bomb symbol and werk nummer are just visible) and to the left, the rear part of the canopy and pilot's head armour.

Opposite: Streich in the cockpit of his Fw 190. He was killed in Fw 190 A-5 werk nummer 840189 which crashed near the airfield at Caen-Carpiquet.

One that almost made it to Manston was this Fw 190 A-5, werk nummer 5259 White R, of 5./Schnellkampfgeschwader 10. Shot down by Typhoons of 609 Squadron attacking Margate on the afternoon of 1 June 1943, it crashed at Westwood south of Margate, killing Unteroffizier Otto Zugenrücker.

Opposite above: Another Jabo landed in error at an RAF airfield in on 20 May 1943. Unteroffizier Heinz Ehrhardt of 2./Schnellkampfgeschwader 10, flying Fw 190 A-4, werk nummer 45843 Red 9, landed at RAF Manston in Kent. Again, the spinner was half white-half green, the rudder yellow and the whole aircraft had its normal camouflage liberally smeared with lamp black.

Opposite below: PM679 was an Fw 190 A-5, werk nummer 2596 White 6, of 1./Schnellkampfgeschwader 10. It also landed at Manston on 20 June 1943, its pilot, Unteroffizier Werner Öhne, having become lost. The underside of cowling and rudder were yellow, spinner dark green and the standard camouflage smeared with lamp black. It also had the stammkennzeichen CL+QH. After being given RAF markings and evaluated by the Royal Aircraft Establishment, it went to the Air Fighting Development Unit at RAF Wittering in July 1943. It suffered smoke in the cockpit on 25 June 1944 and was badly damaged in the resulting forced landing, after which it was struck off charge.

Clearly Werner Öhne's A-5, werk nummer 2596 White 6, with hastily-applied RAF markings.

Opposite above: PE882, formerly Fw 190 A-4, werk nummer 7155 Yellow H, captured at West Malling on 17 April 1943.

Opposite below: Although hard to make out, this is also believed to be PE882 now sporting a P for prototype.

The remains of Fw 190 A-5, werk nummer 840042 Yellow 12, of 3./Schnellkampfgeschwader 10. Damaged by a Mosquito of 85 Squadron near West Malling on 22 June 1943, Unteroffizier Franz Kahlhammer made it as far as Amiens and then lost control coming into land.

Opposite above: Heinz Ehrhardt's A-4, werk nummer 5843, now with serial PN799.

Opposite below: PE882 seen here at RNAS Yeovilton in late 1943.

The starboard wing hit the ground, then the port wing and engine hit the ground, ripping off the engine.

The lamp-blacked tail showing werk nummer 840042. The pilot had a cut over his left eye and a bump on his forehead.

Opposite: Unteroffizier Bogdahn Faul of 3./Schnellkampfgeschwader 10 in front of Yellow 9. Fahl was probably shot down by anti-aircraft fire on 26 November 1943 whilst flying an Fw 190 G-3, werk nummer 160419 PP+SO; he is still listed as missing.

Unteroffizier Artur Lembach of 2./Schnellkampfgeschwader 10 in front of Red 7. Lembach was shot down and killed by a Mosquito of 85 Squadron east of Dunkirk on 24 August 1943 whilst flying Fw 190 A-5 werk nummer 840010; the code is not known.

Unteroffizier Paul Ebbinghaus of 3./Schnellkampfgeschwader 10. He was shot down and killed by friendly fire near Beauvais on 8 May 1943 whilst flying in an Arado Ar 96.

Unteroffizier Otto Heinrich had been a successful Stuka pilot, having joined 8./Stukageschwader 77 in the summer of 1941. He would be credited with destroying thirty-five tanks, fourteen artillery pieces, sixteen anti-aircraft guns, an armoured train, four trains and a torpedo boat. He was awarded the Ehrenpokal in April 1942 and the Deutsches Kreuz in Gold in November 1942 before converting to the Fw 190 and joining 3./Schnellkampfgeschwader 10. He would then be credited with shooting down three Lancasters on 4 May 1944 but was then shot down by anti-aircraft fire while attacking Portsmouth on 22 May 1944 in Fw 190 G-8, werk nummer 190092 Yellow 3. His body would be washed ashore in France and on 20 July 1944, he was posthumously awarded the Ritterkreuz.

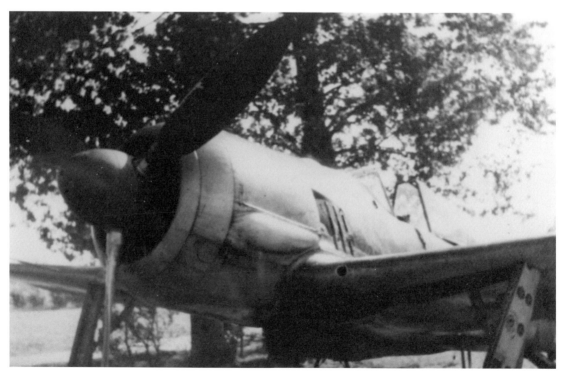

Clearly White 1 but strangely there appears to be a horizontal bar after the fuselage cross. Note the lack of lamp-black camouflage.

Opposite above: Believed to have been taken during the Normandy invasion, this is thought to be White 1 of 1./Schnellkampfgeschwader 10. By June 1944, I./Schnellkampfgeschwader 10 was flying Fw 190 G-3s or G-8s. The G-3 was based on the A-5 but with two MG 151/20 and intended for long-range Jabo missions. The G-8 was similar but based on the A-8.

Opposite below: White 1 hidden under the trees away from Allied aircraft.

The front aircraft has exhaust dampers for night missions. The spinner appears to be a third white.

Opposite above: A well-hidden Jabo at the time of the Normandy invasion. This is believe to be an A-8 variant ready-fitted with drop tanks.

Opposite below: 250kg bomb and drop tanks loaded. Note the two-tone spinner.

Opposite: Loading what appears to be a massive 1,000kg bomb on an Fw 190 G of Nachtschlachtgruppe 20; I./Schnellkampfgeschwader 10 became III./Kampfgeschwader 51 in August 1944 and then Nachtschlachtgruppe 20 in November 1944.

Well and truly hidden at Tours-West is this Fw 190 from I./Schnellkampfgeschwader 10.

RECONNAISSANCE

The Fw 190 A-3 werk nummer 300 was the first example to carry one RB 50/30 and one RB 75/30 camera behind the pilot, the lenses protected by a small fairing underneath the fuselage. The production versions of the A-3/U4 carried two RB 12.5/7x9 cameras seen here, as well as a robot camera in the port wing.

Opposite: Leutnant Johannes Settgast in the cockpit of his Fw 190 A-4/U4 of 2./Nahaufklärungsgruppe 13. He joined the unit as it was forming at Jüterbog-Damm in the late summer of 1942 and after converting from the Arado Ar 96 to the Bf 109 he first flew the Fw 190 on 24 September 1942. 2./Nahaufklärungsgruppe 13 moved to St Brieuc in western France mid-February 1943. He then flew his first operational flight on 21 February 1943.

Pilots celebrating the 500th sortie of 2./Nahaufklärungsgruppe 13. The pilot holding the placard is believed to be Oberleutnant Ludwig Klink and to his right, the Staffelkapitän Hauptmann Roland Eckerscham. Note the distinctively-camouflaged Fw 190 in the background which has the 2./Nahaufklärungsgruppe 13 emblem on the cowling.

Opposite: Fw 190 A-4s of 2./Nahaufklärungsgruppe 13 photographed at Jüterbog-Damm on 6 October 1942, presumably the date when it was first declared as an Fw 190 unit. The Gruppe was commanded by Major Hans-Friedrich Schultze-Moderow and 2 Staffel initially by Hauptmann Karl-Heinz Ebeling.

Johannes Settgast sitting in an Fw 190 A-3. He first flew this actual aircraft on 7 March 1943.

2./Nahaufklärungsgruppe 13 at Jüterbog-Damm, 6 October 1942. The aircraft carried black fuselage markings, the only one visible being Black 4.

Interesting view of Johannes Settgast in the cramped cockpit of his Fw 190.

The distinctive 2./Nahaufklärungsgruppe 13 badge – the eagle is believed to have been red or grey, the waves blue and the cliffs black.

What would appear to be a parachute exercise at St Brieuc, 1943. The Fw 190 on the left is coded Black 3. In late 1943, the numerals were changed to red. Recce missions were normally carried out in pairs.

Opposite: Oberleutnant Heinz Meyer and Oberleutnant Herbert Sell. Sell would be shot down flying Fw 190 A-4, werk nummer 0367 Black 9, on 15 October 1943 by a Typhoon of 266 Squadron together with Oberleutnant Volkmer Klein who was flying Fw 190 A-4, werk nummer 0697 Black 11. Both were killed.

Pilots of 2./Nahaufklärungsgruppe 13 at St Brieuc, spring 1943. Left to right: Leutnant Johannes Settgast, Oberleutnant Herbert Sell (+ 15 October 1943), Oberleutnant Ludwig Klink (+ 24 July 1944), and Feldwebel Egon Güttler. All four would be awarded the Ehrenpokal, and Settgast and Klink the Deutsches Kreuz in Gold. Klink was also credited with shooting down three aircraft whilst with 2./Nahaufklärungsgruppe 13.

Pilots of 2./Nahaufklärungsgruppe 13 in 1944. Left to right: Feldwebel Wittmer, Oberfeldwebel Hans Riewe, Oberfähnrich Horst Barnewald, Oberfeldwebel Fröse, and ?. All appear to have survived the war.

Opposite above: Fw 190 A-5s of 2./Nahaufklärungsgruppe 13, possibly photographed at Dinard in early 1944. Unfortunately no codes can been seen and the unit badges are not in evidence but spinners appear to be red. 2./Nahaufklärungsgruppe 13 would continue to use A-3 and A-4 variants into 1944 but would then operate Bf 109 G-6s, and Fw 190 G-2s and F-8s.

Opposite below: In April 1944, 2./Nahaufklärungsgruppe 13 was operating out of Cuers-Pierrefeu near Toulon where this photograph was taken. Note the distinctive camouflage on Red 4 which has no werk nummer or unit badge visible. Just visible underneath the fuselage below the numeral is the fairing for the cameras.

A war reporter interviewing pilots from 2./Nahaufklärungsgruppe 13 after a mission, Dinard, March 1944. Third from left is Oberleutnant Arnold 'Hein' Grosser who would be killed in an accident on 30 May 1944 when his Bf 109 G-8, werk nummer 710124 Yellow 4, crashed near Laval. By this time he was with 3./Nahaufklärungsgruppe 13.

Celebrating Hauptmann Roland Eckescham's birthday, St Brieuc, 18 November 1943. He had also been awarded the Ehrenpokal as Staffelkapitän on 1 November 1943 and would be awarded the Deutsches Kreuz in Gold in 1945 and survived the war. Note the 2./Nahaufklärungsgruppe 13 Fw 190 in the background.

THE MEDITERRANEAN

Photographed at Bari in 1942, this appears to be an A-1 on its way to a unit. It still has the factory codes, last two letters LH, but the theatre band in white has been applied.

Opposite: Photographed in Italy in 1943 is this Fw 190 of Schnellkampfgeschwader 10 coded White 8. Presumably it is either from II or IV./Schnellkampfgeschwader 10 on its way south as I./Schnellkampfgeschwader 10 remained in France whilst III./Schnellkampfgeschwader 10, formerly III./Zerstörergeschwader 2, was already in theatre, commanded by Hauptmann Fritz Schröter, formerly of 10./Jagdgeschwader 2.

An Fw 190 presumably from II./Schnellkampfgeschwader 10. It is carrying a single AB250-2/224 SD1 container which held 224 SD1 anti-personnel bomblets. Because of the dust, a ground crewman helps the pilot to taxi.

Opposite above: A burnt-out Fw 190 A-5 of IV./Schnellkampfgeschwader 10 at Marsa del Oro, Sicily after at air attack, 7 July 1943. It is believed that this aircraft was usually flown by the Staffelkapitän of 13./Schnellkampfgeschwader 10, Oberleutnant Leopold Wenger. It is possibly werk nummer 1501430.

Opposite below: Oberleutnant Fritz Holzapfel, formerly of 9./Jagdgeschwader 2, was now with 13./Schnellkampfgeschwader 10 and is photographed here at Gerbini. He was killed in action attacking Augusta on 19 July 1943 in an Fw 190 A-5, werk nummer 840051.

Opposite above: Leutnant Helmut Wenk of 5./Schnellkampfgeschwader 10 taking off from Crotone on 1 August 1943 to attack an ammunition dump at Nicosia in Sicily during which his aircraft was badly damaged by anti-aircraft fire. He is possibly flying A-5 werk nummer 181530. Two aircraft failed to return.

Opposite below: Another A-5 Jabo taxiing out. The aircraft is carrying a 500kg bomb and has a white theatre tail band.

The scene of another Allied air attack, this time Crotone in July 1943. The remains of an Fw 190 in the foreground, a Ju 88 in the background. The possible date is 27 July 1943.

Opposite: An A-5 laden with a 500kg bomb. It has the white theatre band, Black H and the last two letters of the stammkennzeichen are SY.

Leutnant Helmut Wenk of 5./Schnellkampfgeschwader 10 in the cockpit of his A-4.

This accident to a 5./Schnellkampfgeschwader 10 Fw 190 A-5 appears to have happened taking off from Crotone and the pilot was uninjured. Some records say this was 27 July 1943, others that it was werk nummer 181706 on 14 August 1943, and flown by Leutnant Helmut Wenk.

Opposite above: Possibly an Fw 190 G-3 photographed in the Mediterranean. Again, it has the theatre band and last two letters of the stammkennzeichen HR. Armourers are struggling with a 500kg bomb.

Opposite below: Pilots of 5./Schnellkampfgeschwader 10 planning a mission, Crotone, July 1943. Left to right: Oberfeldwebel Ernst Rehwoldt (+ 15 August 1943), ?, Feldwebel Rudi Riepelsiep (+ 1 August 1943), Leutnant Walter Klein, Unteroffizier Thrun (+ 1943?), ?.

Fw 190 A-5, werk nummer 1319 Red F, found by Allied troops at Protville, Tunisia, in 1943. The aircraft appears to have hit the ground with the propeller windmilling. It also has desert filters for the intakes.

Opposite above: From November 1942 to March 1943, II./Jagdgeschwader 2 operated in the Mediterranean. This aircraft seen in its protective revetment is believed to be from this unit.

Opposite below: Photographed at San Pietro October–November 1942 are this Reggiane 2001 of 2°Gruppo Autonomo CT 358a Squadrigila (left) and two Fw 190s of II./Jagdgeschwader 2. The Gruppe later moved to Ciampino in November 1942.

Leutnant Kurt Bühligen, Staffelkapitän of 4./Jagdgeschwader 2, in his White 11 in North Africa. His last kill over France was his 28th, a Spitfire on 19 August 1942 and by the time his Gruppe left the Mediterranean in March 1943, it had risen to sixty-eight, his 68th being a P-38 on 12 March 1943.